3/06

19.95

D0745506

The Life and Times of

NERO

Mitchell Lane
PUBLISHERS

P.O. Box 196
Hockessin, Delaware 19707

The Life and Times of

NERO

Jim Whiting

Printing   1   2   3   4   5   6   7   8

Library of Congress Cataloging-in-Publication Data

Whiting, Jim, 1943–
    The life and times of Nero / by Jim Whiting.
        p. cm. — (Biography from ancient civilizations)
    Includes bibliographical references and index.
    ISBN 1-58415-349-0 (library bound)
    1. Nero, Emperor of Rome, 37–68—Juvenile literature. 2. Emperor—Rome—Biography—Juvenile literature. 3. Rome—History—Nero, 54–68—Juvenile literature. I. Title. II. Series.
DG285.W48 2005
937'.07—dc22

                                                                        2004024603

ABOUT THE AUTHOR: Jim Whiting has been a journalist, writer, editor, and photographer for more than 20 years. In addition to a lengthy stint as publisher of *Northwest Runner* magazine, Mr. Whiting has contributed articles to the *Seattle Times*, *Conde Nast Traveler*, *Newsday*, and *Saturday Evening Post*. He has written numerous books for Mitchell Lane in a variety of series. He has also edited more than 100 Mitchell Lane titles. A great lover of classical music and ancient history, he has written many books for young adults, including *The Life and Times of Irving Berlin* and *The Life and Times of Julius Caesar* (Mitchell Lane). He lives in Washington state with his wife and two teenage sons.

PUBLISHER'S NOTE: This story is based on the author's extensive research, which he believes to be accurate. Documentation of such research is contained on page 47.

The internet sites referenced herein were active as of the publication date. Due to the fleeting nature of some web sites, we cannot guarantee they will all be active when you are reading this book.

BIOGRAPHY FROM
ANCIENT CIVILIZATIONS
LEGENDS, FOLKLORE, AND STORIES OF ANCIENT WORLDS

The Life and Times of

NERO

*For Your Information

This bust of Nero shows him when he was still a teenager. It was probably made soon after he became emperor of Rome. He was just sixteen when he ascended to the throne.

CHAPTER
ONE

I AM THE CHAMPION

The Olympic Games are the world's most famous sports event. Every four years, the globe's top athletes compete against each other in the city that has earned the right to host them. Millions of spectators eagerly watch in person or on television. An Olympic gold medal is the world's most prestigious sports award.

The Olympics date back more than 2,700 years. There are some obvious differences between modern and ancient Games. Back then, the Games were always held in the Greek village of Olympia rather than circulating through different cities. There was, of course, no television. Instead of gold medals, winners took home olive wreaths. But one thing was the same: The Olympics were just as important then as they are now.

Winning an Olympic championship was perhaps the highest honor an ancient Greek could achieve. Champions were often set up for the rest of their lives by their grateful and adoring hometowns. The Olympics were even used as a means of measuring time.

"Regardless of war and natural disaster, the Games went on at Olympia, every four years in high summer, each celebration marking the start of a new 'Olympiad,'" writes classicist Edward Champlin.

This picture shows a small section of the ruins of Olympia, Greece. For more than 1,000 years, the Olympic Games were held here. Spectators would travel hundreds of miles to enjoy the athletic contests and religious rituals.

"From the third century B.C. onward, all Greek chronology was based on or synchronized with these four-year Olympiads. Only once was this fundamental cycle of historical time disrupted."[1]

That disruption occurred in the year 67. By that time, Olympia—as well as the rest of Greece—had long been under the control of the Roman Empire. Nero, the Roman emperor, had begun a lengthy trip to Greece the previous year. As part of his tour, he ordered a special edition of the Olympics to be held. It wasn't so that he could watch. He wanted to participate.

Greece had several other athletic festivals with histories almost as long and distinguished as the Olympics. Like the Olympics, they were also held at four-year intervals. Their long-standing legacies didn't mean much to Nero. He ordered all of them to be held at his convenience so that he could compete.

The dates weren't the only tradition that Nero changed. No one thought of him as an athlete. He wasn't a runner, boxer, or wrestler. He was overweight and out of shape. But he considered himself to be an outstanding musician and actor. So he played to his strength. At his command, for the first (and last) time, the Olympics included competition in music. Not surprisingly, Nero won.

He did enter one athletic competition at Olympia: a chariot race. Each end of the course had a very tight 180-degree turn. It was common for the contestants to bump into each other or sometimes even collide head-on.

Racing under these conditions was dangerous enough for the customary two- or four-horse teams. For some reason, Nero demanded a ten-horse race. This requirement nearly proved fatal.

Trying to control ten powerful horses would have been challenging for even a physically fit man. Nero hardly fit that description.

He fell off his chariot early in the race and was very lucky that he wasn't crushed beneath the pounding hooves of the other entrants. The race was halted while the shaken Nero was assisted back into his chariot. Even with this advantage, he wasn't able to finish the course. It didn't matter. The judges still awarded him first place.

He experienced similar "success" wherever he went. No judge who valued his life would have dared to pick anyone else ahead of Nero. Yet Nero liked to pretend that he was not the emperor, that he was competing on a level playing field. He was careful to observe the same rules as everyone else. Whenever he was announced as the winner, he acted completely surprised.

Buoyed by hundreds of these "victories," Nero returned to Rome in triumph. He ordered an elaborate ceremonial parade to honor his accomplishments. A long line of men carried the 1,808 wreaths and

This is the competitors' entrance into the Olympic Stadium. The starting line was at the far end of the field. Thousands of spectators crowded into the banks on each side.

crowns he had won. He followed them, riding in a decorated chariot and displaying the olive wreath from the Olympics.

Thousands of Romans lined the streets. Some of the older ones might have been a little bewildered. In their experience, triumphal parades such as this one were held only to recognize important Roman victories in major battles. This was the first time they'd witnessed a parade that celebrated peaceful pursuits. Confusion aside, they cheered and cheered. Nero must have basked in their enthusiasm. It was perhaps the supreme moment of his life.

Within a year he was dead.

The Olympics

FYI
For Your Info

The Olympic Games began as a religious festival in 776 B.C. in the Greek village of Olympia. At first, they consisted of four days of religious ceremonies, followed by a single sporting event: a dash of about 200 yards. The distance was called a stade, the origin of our word *stadium*. According to legend, the stade was as far as the hero Hercules could run without taking a single breath.

Eventually, several longer running events were added, as were long jumping, discus and javelin throwing, chariot racing, boxing, wrestling, and the pankration, a sort of no-holds-barred hand-to-hand combat in which entrants were sometimes killed. All the competitors were men, who competed naked.

The Olympics were held every four years. If there was fighting among the Greek city-states during that time, a truce would be declared so that everyone could travel to Olympia in safety.

Once they arrived there, the spectators—by some estimates, up to 70,000 or even more—were packed tightly together. Because there was hardly any housing for travelers, everyone except the very wealthy lived in tiny tents or in the open. Bathing and sanitary facilities were almost nonexistent.

Elite athletes began training nearly a year before the Olympics. Officially, winners received only an olive wreath. But they could count on being supported by their grateful home cities, often for the rest of their lives.

With the rise of Christianity in the Roman Empire—of which Greece had become a part—the Olympics were finally banned in A.D. 393 because they honored pagan gods. Earthquakes and floods during the succeeding centuries buried the site, and the Olympics were virtually forgotten.

In the early 1890s, a group of English and French aristocrats headed by Baron Pierre de Coubertin decided to revive the Olympics. The first modern Olympic Games were held in Athens, Greece, in 1896. About 250 athletes from 14 countries attended. Today, thousands of athletes from nearly every country on the globe take part.

11

Virtually all of the land south of the Danube River and west of the Rhine River in this map was part of the Roman Empire at the time that Nero became emperor. His birthplace of Antium can be seen just south of Rome. Olympia, the site of the Olympic Games that he dominated, is at the bottom center of the map.

CHAPTER
TWO

THE TEENAGED EMPEROR

The future emperor was born on December 15, A.D. 37, in the Italian resort town of Antium, present-day Anzio. At his birth he was known as Lucius Domitius Ahenobarbus (LOO-see-us doe-MEE-tee-us uh-hee-no-BAHR-bus). His father was Gnaeus Domitius Ahenobarbus (NIE-us doe-MEE-tee-us un-hee-no-BAHR-bus), a man with a somewhat grisly reputation. The family name meant "bronze beard." According to many people, the family's hearts were made of another metal: lead.

Gnaeus was a swindler. He cheated people who loaned him money. He was accused of treason. Once he killed a freedman in cold blood because the man wouldn't drink with him. He gouged out another man's eyes for saying something he didn't like. He deliberately ran over a small boy in his chariot.

Lucius's mother was Agrippina (AG-rih-PIH-nuh). As we might say today, she had issues. She was descended from Augustus Caesar, the first and—according to most historians—the greatest Roman emperor. Despite all of Augustus's impressive public accomplishments, much of his personal life revolved around identifying a male heir to succeed him because he had no natural-born sons of his own. As a result, a bewildering sequence of marriages involving him, his daughter Julia, and Mark Antony, his primary enemy during his rise to power, created a group of relatives with similar bloodlines and mutual antagonisms. Agrippina's grandmother, for example, was Augustus's daughter Julia. Her grandfather was one of Augustus's stepsons. With so much power at stake, Augustus's descendents often dealt harshly with each other. Agrippina almost certainly had firsthand experience with some harsh events involving her immediate family. Her mother was arrested, beaten so severely that she lost one eye, and eventually starved herself to death. Two of her brothers were also arrested. One committed suicide in jail. The other was murdered. Her third brother, Caligula, was mentally unstable.

Gnaeus and Agrippina were distantly related. Agrippina was Augustus's grandniece, while Gnaeus's grandmother was Augustus's sister Antonia. With this family background, it's no wonder that Roman biographer Suetonius wrote that when Nero was born, his "horoscope at once occasioned many ominous predictions; and a significant comment was made by his father in reply to the congratulations of his friends: namely, that any child born to himself and Agrippina was bound to have a detestable nature and become a public danger."[1]

The "danger" part of the prediction would take years to surface. The "public" part was evident right away. Lucius's family tree guaranteed that he would be in the public eye. He was the great-grandnephew of Augustus Caesar. In turn, Augustus had been the grandnephew of Julius Caesar. This heritage provided Lucius with a direct link to Rome's two most famous men.

In the turbulent world of Roman politics, that link was both a blessing and a curse. Julius Caesar had come to power following a bloody civil war. Fearing that he was growing too powerful, a group of Roman senators assassinated him in 44 B.C. Augustus Caesar, eighteen at the time, emerged with virtually absolute power thirteen years later. He used his power to stabilize Rome for more than forty years. With his reign and the reign of his stepson and successor Tiberius, Rome had enjoyed relative peace for nearly seven decades.

That was about to end. Tiberius's successor as emperor was Caligula, who came to power in 37, the same year that Nero was born. At first all went well, but it soon became apparent that Caligula had no skill in governing. A number of his actions, such as trying to have his favorite horse appointed to high public office, suggested that he was insane. With some justification, Caligula thought that many people were conspiring against him. In his mind, these conspirators included his sisters. One of them was Agrippina—Lucius's mother. He ordered her banished from Rome.

Tiberius was Augustus Caesar's stepson. He was a successful military commander before becoming emperor when Augustus Caesar died in A.D. 14. Tiberius ruled until his death 23 years later.

Soon afterward, Lucius's father died. Lucius, still a toddler, should have inherited a third of his father's estate. The scheming co-heir Caligula confiscated it.

With his father dead and his mother in exile, the little boy could have easily perished. Fortunately, his aunt Domitia Lepida took him in, and a male ballet dancer and a barber cared for him. Even so, it wasn't a very comfortable existence.

Caligula was murdered by his own guards in 41. Few people grieved for his loss. His successor was his uncle Claudius. By most reports, Claudius governed well.

For Lucius, Claudius's accession had several immediate benefits. The new emperor restored the boy's inheritance. He also allowed Agrippina to return. She quickly remarried. In what may have been a foreshadowing of the future, her new husband—a very rich man—died

Caligula became emperor in A.D. 37 at the age of 25. While he was popular at first, he soon showed signs of mental instability and abused his power. He was murdered by his own guards less than four years after assuming power.

in 44. His death conveniently allowed Agrippina to receive all his wealth.

For the next few years, Lucius appears to have enjoyed some stability in his personal life. One of Rome's most respected citizens, Asconius Labeo, was appointed as his guardian. Two of the city's best tutors took over his education. Meanwhile, the boy probably was not aware of what was going on in his mother's scheming mind. She wanted her son to become emperor. Virtually everything she did was with that goal in mind.

Lucius made his first public appearance in 47. That was the 800th anniversary of the legendary founding of Rome by the twins Romulus and Remus. Lucius was introduced as the representative of the Augustan line.

The 801st anniversary of Rome's founding—the year 48—got off to a rocky start. Claudius's young wife (his third), Valeria Messalina, had frequently been unfaithful to him. Now she tried to marry another man and replace Claudius with him. Claudius forced her to commit suicide and vowed that he would never marry again.

The vow didn't last long. Claudius, in his late fifties, soon found another wife—Agrippina. She was also his niece. In order to marry her, Claudius had to get special permission from the Senate. There was a practical reason for their approval. Because of her relationship with the Caesars, it would be potentially dangerous if she married into a different family.

Agrippina probably didn't need any convincing. Now that she was married to the Roman emperor, her scheming moved into high gear.

She arranged for her son to become engaged to Octavia, Claudius's daughter. Then she talked Claudius into adopting Lucius, even though he already had a natural-born son named Britannicus, who was three years younger than Lucius. As a result of the adoption, which took place in 50, Lucius became known as Nero Claudius Caesar Drusus Germanicus.

Nothing could be too good for Agrippina's only child. She wanted Seneca, the most learned man in the Roman Empire, to serve as his tutor. Seneca was regarded as the best public speaker of his day. He was also a philosopher, a playwright, an essayist, and a member of the Senate. Several years earlier, he had been romantically involved with one of Agrippina's sisters. Messalina sent the lovers into exile. Seneca must have been aware that he was setting foot into a hornet's nest by accepting Agrippina's invitation, but the opportunity to come back to Rome was too great to pass up.

Seneca did his best. He tried to instill a sense of morality into his pupil. He worked to make Lucius a good public speaker. He even wrote the speeches that the boy delivered to the Senate and the Roman public.

In 51, when he was thirteen, Nero became entitled to wear the *toga virilis*. It was a special garment that, like the Jewish bar mitzvah ceremony, signified that its wearer was now officially a man. Claudius named him *princeps iuventutis*, or "leader of youth," meaning he was someone to be admired and emulated. Soon afterward, Nero made his first speech to the Roman Senate. He thanked Claudius for bestowing so many honors on him.

Two years later Nero, at fifteen, married Octavia. His new wife was two years younger. The marriage was almost certainly doomed from the start. Both bride and groom were too young to marry, yet neither one could say no. They were trapped by the Roman tradition of arranged marriages, which was especially rigid for aristocrats.

Events began moving swiftly toward Agrippina's goal. The unsuspecting Claudius made a brief trip away from Rome and left his

Valeria Messalina married Claudius when she was about 16 and he was 48. She had a reputation for scheming to get rid of people she disliked. She even tried to get rid of Claudius. That was a mistake. Claudius had her killed when he learned of the plot.

stepson in charge. By all accounts, Nero was successful during this brief administration.

To anyone looking at Nero from the outside, his situation must have seemed enviable. The reality was different. As Richard Holland notes, "Having been elevated to the effective position of heir and presumed successor, he either fulfilled his mother's ambition and became emperor—or he would be killed."[2]

His mother put him through a major test. She accused his aunt Lepida—who had given him a home while his mother was in exile—of practicing magic, a serious charge at that time. Agrippina may have believed that Lepida was trying to supplant her and Nero with Britannicus—who in the confused web of Roman politics was Lepida's grandson. The trial forced the fifteen-year-old Nero into making a horrible choice: between his mother and the woman who had taken care of him when he was a lonely three-year-old and desperately needed someone. Nero chose his mother. He testified against Lepida. She was executed.

For Agrippina, getting rid of Lepida was just a warm-up. Britannicus was now thirteen and on the verge of assuming the *toga virilis* himself. She knew that Claudius had changed his will. A hint of the new contents may have been revealed when he publicly embraced Britannicus, telling him that putting on the *toga virilis* "will at last provide Rome with a true-born Caesar."[3] Just as ominously, he bragged to some of his drinking buddies that he seemed fated to marry disobedient women—and then to punish them. These signs must have conveyed the same message to Agrippina: Claudius was about to dump her and her son.

What happened next is certain. On the evening of October 12, 54, Claudius devoured a dish of cooked mushrooms, one of his favorite foods. It was his last meal. Within a few hours he was dead.

The cause of death is uncertain. However, nearly everyone at the time believed that Agrippina had secured the services of Locusta, a woman famous for her skill with poisons.

No one knows if Nero had any direct connection with the death of Claudius. A relatively new Roman tradition had resulted in dead emperors being treated as gods. About a century after Claudius's death, historian Dio Cassius sarcastically noted, "Nero declared mushrooms to be the food of the gods, since Claudius by means of a mushroom had become a god."[4]

Regardless of how Claudius had died, Nero and Agrippina didn't waste any time grieving for him. The following morning, Nero stepped outside the palace. A cheer greeted him as the new emperor. The next step was to secure the loyalty of the Praetorian Guard. Created by Augustus, this was a force of several thousand elite soldiers who were charged with protecting the emperor. Nero and his mother promised each man several years' wages if they supported him. They all accepted the offer.

The Senate, which had never liked Claudius, also fell into line. It helped that Nero said all the right things to them. But that shouldn't have been surprising. Seneca had taught him well, and Seneca wasn't the only one pushing all the right buttons. The sixteen-year-old was also being influenced by Burrus, the head of the Praetorian Guard. And of course there was always his mother.

At first, these three influences—Agrippina, Seneca, and Burrus— produced a period of peace and prosperity. The government was efficient and stable. The army was doing a good job of protecting the borders of the empire. Food and trade goods flowed easily.

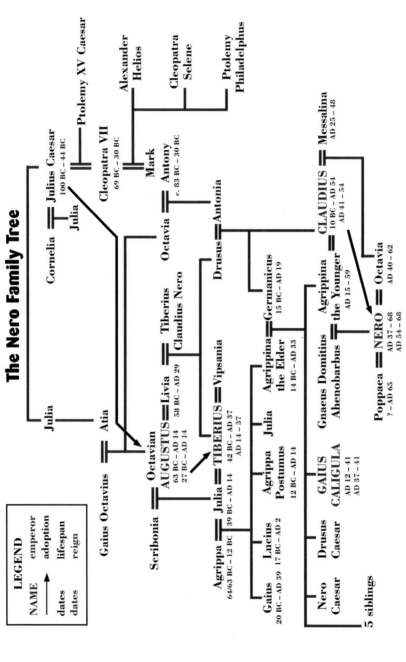

The Nero Family Tree

Julia

Cornelia ══ Julius Caesar
                100 BC – 44 BC

Ptolemy XV Caesar

Julia

Cleopatra VII
69 BC – 30 BC

Mark Antony
c. 83 BC – 30 BC

Alexander Helios

Cleopatra Selene

Ptolemy Philadelphus

Gaius Octavius ══ Atia

Octavia ══ Drusus ══ Antonia

Tiberius Claudius Nero

CLAUDIUS ══ Messalina
10 BC – AD 54   AD 25 – 48
AD 41 – 54

Scribonia ══ Octavian

AUGUSTUS ══ Livia
63 BC – AD 14   58 BC – AD 29
27 BC – AD 14

Agrippina Germanicus
the Elder   15 BC – AD 19
14 BC – AD 33

Agrippina the Younger
AD 15 – 59

Octavia
AD 40 – 62

Julia ══ TIBERIUS ══ Vipsania
39 BC – AD 14   42 BC – AD 37
                    AD 14 – 37

Agrippa ══ Julia
64/63 BC – 12 BC

Gnaeus Domitius Ahenobarbus

Poppaea ══ NERO
? – AD 65   AD 37 – 68
            AD 54 – 68

Gaius
20 BC – AD 39

Lucius
17 BC – AD 2

Agrippa Postumus
12 BC – AD 14

Julia

GAIUS CALIGULA
AD 12 – 41
AD 37 – 41

Nero Caesar

Drusus Caesar

5 siblings

This family tree reveals the complex relationships and intermarriages among the descendents of Julius Caesar and Augustus Caesar that culminated with the birth of Nero. Nero wasn't the only emperor to deal harshly with relatives who might pose a threat to his power. Augustus ordered Ptolemy XV Caesar, Julius Caesar's son with Cleopatra, to be strangled to eliminate a potential rival.

Augustus Caesar

Gaius Octavius, or Octavian, as he was more commonly known, was born in 63 B.C. His mother was the niece of Julius Caesar, who designated Octavian as his heir shortly before his assassination in 44 B.C.

Several years earlier, Caesar won a bloody civil war. His death threatened new violence. Many senators feared Caesar's close friend Mark Antony. They believed they could use the teenaged Octavian—who now carried the prestige of the Caesar name—to curb Antony's power. Then they would cast the boy aside. Octavian did help defeat Antony. But when Antony joined Lepidus, another supporter of Caesar, Octavian recognized their combined strength and formed an alliance with them. He willingly sacrificed his supporters in the Senate, many of whom were killed.

The three men were too ambitious to work together. With the help of his friend Agrippa, an excellent general, Octavian defeated Lepidus in 36 B.C. and Antony five years later. He was now the most powerful man in Rome. He knew he had to be careful how he used his power or he too could be assassinated. It helped that Romans were tired of decades of conflict. They wanted peace. Octavian gave it to them. In 27 B.C., the Senate honored him with the new name of Augustus Caesar.

Augustus wanted a male heir. Since he had no natural-born son of his own, he ordered his daughter Julia to marry three times. One marriage was to his friend Agrippa, which produced two boys whom Augustus adopted as his heirs. But they died as young men. Then he adopted his stepson Tiberius, who became emperor when Augustus died in A.D. 14.

The line of succession was even more complicated because Augustus's sister had married Mark Antony, and Augustus's other stepson, Drusus, had married Mark Antony's daughter. The result was a number of relatives who had a claim to the throne. With so much power at stake, the various claimants—including Nero—became ruthless in dealing with their potential rivals.

This statue shows Agrippina symbolically placing the emperor's crown on Nero's head. The harmony between mother and son quickly disappeared. After several years of increasing strain, Nero ordered her to be killed.

CHAPTER
THREE

BECOMING INDEPENDENT

Following the traumatic events of his early childhood, Nero had never known anything other than the most luxurious surroundings. He had no experience in the real world. Even worse, he had virtually no sense of morality in spite of Seneca's best efforts to teach him otherwise.

Beneath the seeming peace and prosperity of Nero's first years, his deficiencies were already at work to undermine his reign. They became apparent all too soon.

One of the main deficiencies was his reliance on his mother. Now that she had achieved a sort of royal "triple crown"—sister of one emperor (Caligula), wife of a second (Claudius), and mother of a third (Nero)—Agrippina started to eliminate other descendents of Augustus so that they couldn't become rivals in the future. Historian Michael Grant notes the degree of their eventual success: "Whatever sections of the population found the reign of Nero enjoyable (and they were many), those members of the aristocracy who had any blood of the Caesars in their veins were not among their number. Indeed, none of them survived it."[1]

Nero became directly involved in this purge. Convinced that Britannicus presented a threat, Nero decided to get rid of him a year after he became emperor. According to a widely circulated story, Britannicus took a poisoned drink at a banquet he and Nero were attending. He instantly went into convulsions and stopped breathing. Nero calmly continued eating. He explained that Britannicus was just having an epileptic fit. When Britannicus didn't revive, Nero ordered the body to be cremated. The remains were buried that very night.

No one has ever proved that Nero actually poisoned him. Certainly there was another type of poison at work: one between Nero and his mother. She had recently shown an interest in Britannicus, which may have reflected a growing split between mother and son. Immediately after Claudius's death, images of Agrippina and Nero had appeared together on coins. Agrippina occupied the dominant position, and the inscription referred to her. Within a few months, the situation was reversed. Nero was the one who was featured. Not long afterward, her image disappeared completely. Like many young men, Nero was probably tired of a dominating mother who wouldn't let go of him.

He was also probably tired of the day-to-day details of administering the western world's largest empire. The real power lay behind the scenes, where Seneca and Burrus worked together in a display of harmony that was rare among the power-hungry Roman elite. Theirs was an ideal combination. As a soldier, Burrus was skilled in keeping the empire's borders safe. Seneca's influence was more in internal affairs.

One of the ways of keeping the general population in order was by providing elaborate, expensive public entertainments. For many years, gladiator combats had been popular. Under Seneca's influence, Nero tried to reduce them and even ordered that no one could be killed. Because the whole point of going to see the gladiators was to watch people being killed, it was a ban that proved impossible to enforce. Even if it had been enforced, Nero found plenty of other ways of entertaining the bloodthirsty Roman public and making himself popular. He continued other entertainments that previous emperors had established. Chariot races that attracted crowds of up to 250,000 featured both the opportunity to bet and the likelihood of bloody collisions. Sometimes Nero would order large public arenas to be flooded so that "naval battles" could be staged. He also funded extravagant theatrical productions.

He built himself a large and expensive palace. It was a larger version of the elegant mansions of Roman aristocrats, and completely different from the modest structure that Augustus Caesar had occupied during his reign. There were dozens of richly decorated public rooms, even more numerous private ones, and elaborate gardens.

Claudius became emperor after the death of Caligula. His most notable accomplishment was adding Britain to the Roman Empire. His death paved the way for Nero to become emperor.

This would have been a remarkable home for anyone. For a teenager, it was probably a case of too much, too soon. He was spoiled by its luxury.

When Augustus Caesar had risen to power, he was very conscious that his predecessor, Julius Caesar, had been assassinated because he had seemed to want too much power. As a result, he was very careful to maintain his public image of a man who had Rome's best interests at heart.

Reaching power several decades later, Nero had no such concerns. He felt that he could do anything he wanted. Even though he was

Octavia was the daughter of Claudius and Valeria Messalina. She and Nero were married when she was only thirteen. Even though she was popular with the Roman people, Nero got rid of her so he could marry another woman.

married to Octavia, he became involved with a woman named Acte. He provided her with several expensive houses and hundreds of slaves. He threw all-night parties and allowed outrageous behavior—in which he happily participated. He also enjoyed putting on costumes and wandering through the streets at night with groups of friends, beating up people for no apparent reason, and destroying property.

He soon distanced himself from government. Much of the day-to-day work was done by thousands of men working in the vast Roman bureaucracy.

He found himself surrounded by sycophants (SIH-kuh-fants), men who told him what he wanted to hear. No one was going to criticize his actions—to his face. That would have been a sure way to get killed.

As his power became greater and greater, he found himself less and less willing to share it with his mother.

Gladiators

Rome had a well-deserved reputation for cruel popular entertainments. These entertainments often took the form of wild animals fighting each other, well-armed men butchering animals, or unarmed men cowering in fright as hungry animals such as lions were released. However, the most famous were fights to the death among gladiators.

Gladiators were almost always slaves, criminals, or prisoners of war. Surprisingly, a few men even volunteered. They all received training in special schools to learn their "trade" before going on public display. Sometimes they fought in pairs, sometimes in large groups.

Gladiatorial combat took place in huge open-air arenas, often with musical accompaniment. The word *arena* has a grim origin. It comes from the word for "sand," which was spread liberally to absorb blood because it was common for dozens or even hundreds of gladiators to die in a single day.

There were several types of gladiators, depending on the amount of armor they wore and their weapons. Some were *retiarii*, or net men, who carried weighted nets to ensnare their opponents. Some carried a small shield and curved sword. Still others wore heavy armor, which helped to protect them but also slowed them down. What they had in common was a very limited life expectancy. They were always a single mistake away from violent death. Often a gladiator would be severely wounded and crumple to the floor of the arena with his adversary standing over him. When that happened, he could appeal to the audience for mercy. If they thought he had fought well, the audience might spare him. If not, he would be killed.

Occasionally a gladiator could survive long enough to become a crowd favorite and enjoy some of the same glamour of modern rock stars. If he continued to do well, he could enjoy something even better. He could be set free—both from his dangerous life as a gladiator and from slavery.

Two scenes of Roman baths. The pictures show the main pool, which was heated. The electric lights in the lower photo indicate that it depicts a modern reconstruction.

CHAPTER FOUR

FROM MURDERER TO MUSICIAN

Even though Agrippina had been out of public view for several years after the death of Britannicus, her influence had not completely disappeared.

"Agrippina was not content to be just one of the most influential individuals in the Roman world," writes Richard Holland. "Having for several years before his accession dictated every waking moment of Nero's life, his mother found it impossible to accept 'No' for an answer. Her response to 'No' was to nag him repeatedly to change his mind, and, if that failed, to try to get her own way by some indirect route."[1]

Her presence created a potentially hazardous situation for Nero. Appearing to agree to his mother's demands could be dangerous in the status-conscious, male-dominated Roman aristocracy. On a more personal level, Nero probably became increasingly resentful of the demands that his mother continued to place on him as he grew older. Her "love" became more and more suffocating.

At first, his efforts to solve his "mother problem" seemed almost silly. He childishly threatened to give up his throne and move away from Rome. He took away her bodyguards. He deluged her with people bearing petty lawsuits. He ordered his friends to walk or ride past her estate and shout insults at her.

In 59, Nero decided on a permanent solution. He plotted a series of attempts to kill her that might seem almost comical if they didn't involve murder. He hired Locusta, the poisoner. Agrippina was familiar with Locusta's methods, so her efforts were in vain. He hired an architect to build a bedroom ceiling that would collapse on her. That didn't work either.

Then he hired a man to construct a special boat. It contained luxurious quarters for Agrippina. The ceiling was packed with lead weights that would fall on her, crushing her. As a bonus, the weights would also poke holes in the boat's hull, causing it to sink and destroy any evidence of foul play. All was in readiness. Under the pretext of reconciliation, he invited her to visit him at his seaside villa. After the visit was over, she departed on the boat. When the weights fell, the high sides of the couch on which she was lying took most of the force. Though stunned, Agrippina managed to escape from the wreck and swim to some nearby fishing boats. Her survival threw Nero into a panic.

Nero decided on a direct approach. He ordered some men to stab her to death. When they succeeded, he burned the body. He explained that she had been planning to assassinate him. He ordered a public thanksgiving for his "deliverance" from this "disaster."

Agrippina turned out to be too clever for her own good. To elevate her son to the throne, she had plotted and schemed endlessly, killing anyone who stood in the way of her ambition. As we might say today, she'd created a monster. The son for whom she had committed murder had in turn murdered her.

Freed from her embarrassing and nagging presence, Nero began following the passion that would consume much of his energy for the rest of his life. He wanted to become a great actor and musician. His mother had essentially handed him the Roman Empire. Perhaps he wanted to achieve something on his own. The goal of receiving applause from adoring audiences became important to him.

He threw all his energy into his craft. As Suetonius writes, "Little by little, he began to study and practice himself, and conscientiously undertook all the usual exercises for strengthening and developing the voice. He would lie on his back with a slab of lead on his chest, use enemas and emetics to keep down his weight, and refrain from eating apples and every other food considered deleterious [damaging] to the vocal cords. Ultimately, though his voice was feeble and husky, he was pleased enough with his progress to begin to nurse theatrical ambitions."[2]

These ambitions created a serious problem. To the Roman aristocracy, performing in public was a profession fit only for the lower classes. It was unthinkable and disgraceful that the emperor would stoop to such a level. Yet no one was about to tell Nero that he couldn't keep on doing what had become almost an obsession with him. So Seneca did the best he could. He set up a series of performances with carefully selected audiences whose applause was guaranteed. This "evidence" of success only served to increase the size of Nero's ego, making him believe that he was better than he actually was.

There was another way in which Nero departed from custom. He loved chariot racing. It became almost as much of an obsession as his music. He frequently played with ivory chariots on a large board. Then he went beyond being a spectator and became an actual participant. Even though Nero pointed out that many ancient kings had been skilled charioteers, by this time it was unheard of for aristocrats to drive their own chariots. Slaves normally performed this function. Seneca and Burrus must have shaken their heads in frustration. To avoid as much embarrassment as possible, they set up a private racecourse.

Nero also established a new type of public entertainment. Up to this point, the majority of the lavish public entertainments that Romans enjoyed so much had featured cruelty and killing. Reflecting his new cultural interests, Nero may have had a genuine desire to raise the level of these entertainments. He admired the Greeks because of their cultural heritage, so he modeled his new project—which he called the Neronia—on Greek games such as the Olympics. Held for the first time in the year 60 on October 13—the anniversary of his accession to power—the Neronia included music and poetry in addition to chariot racing and other traditional sports.

To further encourage athletic competition, Nero built a huge new athletic complex in the center of Rome. Nearby he constructed the Baths of Nero, the finest bathhouse in the city. It became a gathering place for Romans of nearly all social classes.

One of the major checks on Nero's excesses ended when Burrus died in 62. Some historians believe that he was poisoned. Seneca, despairing at controlling Nero by himself, gave up and went into voluntary exile. Burrus's successor was Tigellinus, who was willing to go along with Nero's murderous fantasies. He began a reign of terror, in which a number of prominent Romans were accused (often falsely) of treason and conspiracy. They were executed.

Nero wanted to marry his girlfriend, a nineteen-year-old named Poppaea Sabina. She was a beautiful woman who achieved fame for developing a face cream made of bread dough and donkey's milk. She was pregnant with his child.

Officially Nero was still married to Octavia, who was popular because she was the child of Claudius. First he tried a smear campaign against her, but hardly anyone believed the absurd charges that he made. Once again he fell back on the direct approach. He had her banished to a nearby island, where she was murdered. He proudly showed her head to Poppaea. Less than two weeks later he married her. In January 63, she gave birth to a daughter named Claudia. The infant died two months later.

Nero began spending more and more time at his birthplace in Antium. It was there that a messenger arrived on a hot July day in 64 with shocking news. Rome was on fire.

Public Baths

Romans placed a high value on cleanliness. Because only the wealthy could afford to build their own bathing facilities, the city maintained dozens of public bathhouses. Even small towns had at least one or two. In general, bathhouses were limited to women from the time they opened just after dawn until early or mid-afternoon, with the men taking over after that. Admission prices were deliberately set very low so that nearly everyone could afford to use them.

Many bathhouses, especially in Rome itself, were elaborate structures that could accommodate hundreds or even thousands of people at a time. Some were especially luxurious, featuring mirrored walls and pools lined with expensive marble. Bathers would leave their clothes in a changing room. Their first stop would be the steam room or another room with dry heat, similar to a sauna. Then they would step into a large heated pool. After a leisurely soak or invigorating swim, they would pour cold water over themselves to close their pores. To relax even more, they could also hire a person to give them a massage.

Strigil

Since Romans didn't have soap, they cleaned themselves with olive oil. Then they would scrape themselves with a curved bronze device called a strigil, or they would order a slave to do this. The strigil would remove dirt, dead skin, and moisture.

The heat to produce steam and to warm the pools came from huge fires that were maintained by slaves. The hot air was directed through vents under the floors and inside the walls. The areas that surrounded the pools became so hot that patrons had to wear some kind of footwear so that they wouldn't burn their feet.

The bathhouses were more than places to get clean. They served as social centers, where people looked forward to meeting friends and associates, gossiping and conducting business. Many of them also included extensive exercise areas, libraries, gardens, and places to eat.

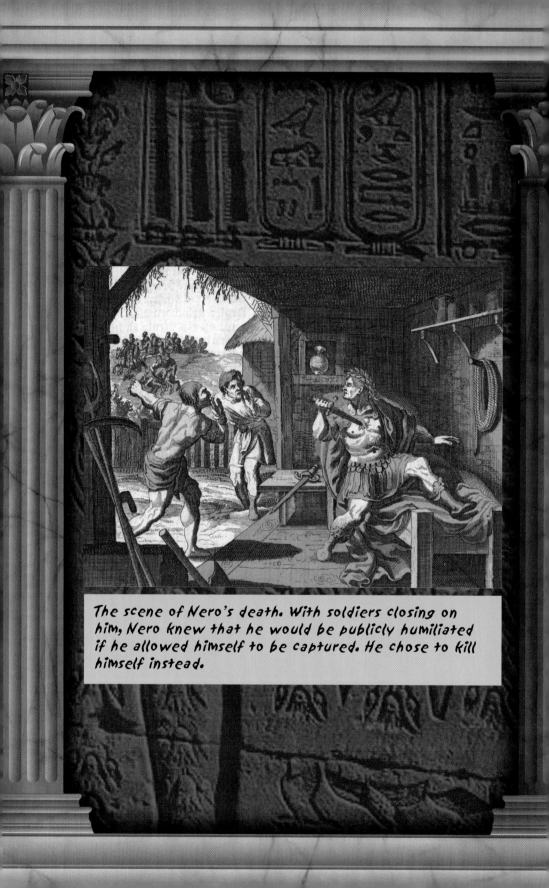

The scene of Nero's death. With soldiers closing on him, Nero knew that he would be publicly humiliated if he allowed himself to be captured. He chose to kill himself instead.

CHAPTER
FIVE

A LONELY DEATH

While many of Rome's public structures were built of marble, most of the rest of the city's buildings were made of wood and packed tightly together. It was a disaster waiting to happen. Now the waiting had ended. A small fire quickly roared out of control. Strong winds carried the flames throughout the city. Although Augustus Caesar had instituted fire brigades to thwart such a disaster, the brigades were overwhelmed by the speed and strength of the fire. It burned for nine days and consumed much of Rome.

Much later, a legend about the event would evolve: Nero fiddled while Rome burned. It is clearly false. Nero couldn't have fiddled because it would be many centuries before the fiddle, or violin, would even be invented. The source of the legend is a story that at the height of the blaze he stood in a tower and recited a poem while accompanying himself on the lyre.

Even that story may have been false. According to most accounts, Nero behaved commendably during the catastrophe. As soon as he learned of the fire, he rushed back to the city from Antium and began directing efforts to combat the blaze. He arranged for temporary accommodations to shelter the thousands of suddenly homeless people and for food to feed them.

On the other hand, he seized much of the burned property, without compensating the owners, and began a massive building program. Part of this seizure seems to have been well intentioned. Even contemporary writers had a grudging admiration for his strict new building regulations to reduce fire hazards in the future. Typically, however, Nero threw away what little goodwill he may have gained when he chose to use part of the seized land to build a monstrous new palace. Most people were shocked at what he called the Golden House.

Suetonius describes some of its features: "The entrance hall was large enough to contain a huge statue of himself, 120 feet high; and the pillared arcade ran for a whole mile. An enormous pool, like a sea, was surrounded by buildings made to resemble cities. . . . Parts of the house were overlaid with gold and studded with precious stones and mother-of-pearl. All the dining-rooms had ceilings of fretted ivory, the panels of which could slide back and let a rain of flowers, or of perfume from hidden sprinklers, shower upon his guests. The main dining-room was circular, and its roof revolved, day and night, in time with the sky. . . . When the palace had been decorated throughout in this lavish style, Nero dedicated it and condescended to remark: 'Good, now I can at last begin to live like a human being.'"[1]

To pay for it, he had to increase taxes. People grumbled. Rumors began circulating. Nero had set the fire himself, people said (looking around carefully to see who might be listening), as a pretext for building this obscenely huge new palace.

When these rumors reached Nero, he decided that he needed a scapegoat, someone else he could blame for starting the fire. He chose a relatively small, obscure religious sect called the Christians. These were Jews who believed a prophet named Jesus, who had been crucified more than thirty years earlier, had been the Christ, or Messiah, promised by the Bible. The Christians kept to themselves, performing a series of mysterious rituals that made them different from other Romans. No one bothered them because they seemed harmless.

That was about to change. Nero blamed them for starting the fire and launched the first organized persecution of Christians. All over Rome, they were rounded up. No punishment was too cruel for Nero's depraved mind. Some were dressed in animal skins and ripped apart by hungry dogs. Others were crucified. Perhaps the most horrible fate came to the ones who were drenched in oil, tied to posts, and then set afire to serve as torches to light pathways at night.

Nero's plan of diversion didn't work. People were shocked at his cruelty. It became one more complaint against his reign.

His reputation declined even further. Up to this time, Nero had confined his musical and theatrical performances to carefully selected private audiences. Now he began performing in public. To Roman aristocrats, it was utterly disgraceful. To Romans who had to endure his performances, it was utterly tedious.

Suetonius reports, "No one was allowed to leave the theatre during his recitals, however pressing the reason. We read of women in the audience giving birth, and of men being so bored with listening and applauding that they furtively dropped down from the wall at the rear, since the gates were kept barred, or shammed [played] dead and were carried away for burial."[2]

Nero was becoming more and more unpopular. In turn, he lashed out against his enemies, real or imagined. In 65, he executed more than fifty senators and army officers when he learned of a plot to overthrow him. One of the condemned men, named Flavius, said, "I hated you . . . I began hating you when you murdered your mother and wife and became a charioteer, actor, and fire-starter."[3]

His old tutor Seneca was another victim. Nero ordered him to commit suicide by cutting his own arteries with a knife.

Not even Poppaea was spared. Again pregnant, she criticized him for coming home late one night. He kicked her and she died from her injuries.

He seemed to be losing touch with reality. He wanted to imitate his ancestors Julius Caesar and Augustus Caesar, both of whom had months named after them. He changed the name of April to Neroneus, though the new name wouldn't last very long. He even tried to rename Rome itself. He wanted it to be known as Neropolis.

A climate of fear enveloped the city. Nero had informers and spies everywhere. More and more people were rounded up and put to death. His relatives were in especial danger. Soon anyone with any connection to the name Caesar was dead.

These harsh measures stirred up even more resentment. The only reason Nero was still in power was that the army supported him. He began to erode that support in 66 when he put Corbulo, probably Rome's most popular general, on trial. Corbulo committed suicide rather than face humiliation. That may have been the last straw. Because Nero had spent virtually all his time in the palace, surrounded by men and women who flattered him and built up his ego, he didn't realize how dependent he was on the army. Certainly he exhibited little if any understanding of his soldiers.

As Phil Grabsky, a historian and director of documentaries about ancient Rome, notes, "He had no rapport with the armies; he had never shared in their campaigns, never visited their camps, paid no attention to their conditions in the provinces, and had recently taken to giving senior army appointments to people he trusted, whatever their qualities or suitability for the post. . . . Nero had made a fatal mistake—alienating the military doomed his reign."[4]

It was typical of Nero's disregard of reality that he chose this dangerous time to make his long trip to Greece. "The Greeks alone are worthy of my efforts, they really listen to music,"[5] he explained.

By this time, Nero's incompetence and ruthlessness were creating widespread dissatisfaction. Nearly everyone in positions of authority felt that their lives were in danger. Rebellion seemed the only route to safety. His long absence during his trip to Greece allowed his enemies to advance their plots. When one of his few remaining loyal supporters urged him to return, he scoffed at the man. There is some evidence that he planned on continuing his travels into Asia, but the Jewish Revolt—which had begun about the time he left for Greece—caused him to return to Rome. Even then, he traveled slowly, basking in the adulation of the crowds that lined the roads as he passed. The enthusiasm that greeted him when he led his triumphant parade may have blinded him to what was really going on.

He got a wakeup call in April 68. The legions in Spain declared Galba, the province's governor, as the emperor and began marching toward Rome. On the verge of panic, Nero tried to organize defensive measures. Hardly anyone responded. He was forced to draft slaves.

Two months later, the news was even worse. Most of his legions refused to support him. Rightfully fearing for his life, he began making hurried plans to flee from the city. He was too late. Just after midnight on June 11, he woke up to find that his personal guard and his friends had deserted him.

His faithful freedman Phaon offered him a hiding place in a villa a few miles outside of town. Panic-stricken, Nero fled into the night with Phaon and three other freedmen and took refuge at the villa. Shortly after dawn, he received a note from the Senate. They had accepted Galba as emperor and declared Nero as a public enemy.

Public enemies were not just killed, they were humiliated. According to one of the freedmen, "He would be led naked through the streets with his neck in a yoke, he would be beaten with rods until he died, and his body would be thrown from the Tarpeian Rock,"[6] a steep cliff overlooking the Roman Forum.

Totally terrified, Nero heard the sound of approaching horses. With the help of his secretary, he pushed a sword into his throat. Moments later he was dead.

The Caesars were gone. The name wasn't. Future Roman emperors would adopt the name Caesar as an honorary title. The title spread to other countries and entered their languages. When dozens of small German states united in the late nineteenth century to form an empire, their leader was known as the kaiser, the German version of *Caesar*. For centuries, the rulers of Russia took the name of czar, which is also derived from *Caesar*. The word is often used today in the United States. For example, the director of the White House Office of National Drug Control Policy is often referred to as the "drug czar," while the Assistant Secretary of Commerce for Manufacturing and Services is nicknamed the "manufacturing czar."

Of more immediate concern to Nero's fellow Romans was that his purge of his relatives had been so complete that he was the only surviving descendant of Augustus. Nero's reign had been bad enough. The circumstances under which he had died—without leaving an heir—were guaranteed to lead to chaos.

The following period of about eighteen months has been given the grim name of "The Year of the Four Emperors" because of the bloodshed that occurred during this time. With the support of his legions, Galba marched on Rome. A good general, he quickly proved to be a bad ruler and lost most of his influence. Otho, a supporter of both Nero and Galba, became enraged when the childless seventy-one-year-old Galba appointed Lucius Calpurnius Piso Frugi Licinianus as his heir. His name was long. His remaining time on earth was short. On January 15, 69, Otho's forces slaughtered Galba, the heir, and a number of advisers. Otho proclaimed himself as the new emperor.

In the meantime, one of the northern provinces had decided that its governor, Vitellius, should become emperor. In a battle on April 16,

Vitellius's forces defeated Otho's troops. Otho committed suicide. The Senate accepted Vitellius as the new emperor.

The killing still wasn't over. A well-respected general named Vespasian had been commanding Roman armies in Judea, dealing with the Jewish Revolt. He left his son Titus behind and hurried back to Rome. In October 69, an army under his command overthrew Vitellius and executed him. Now Vespasian was emperor. He managed to restore order and ruled for ten years. An uneasy peace had returned to Rome.

But no one could forget Nero. Barely thirty at the time of his death, he became one of the most infamous figures in both Roman and world history.

"Nero has remained notorious for two millennia because of a series of extravagant public gestures, usually outrageous, often repellent, always riveting: murdering his mother, killing his pregnant wife in a rage, racing a ten-horse chariot at the Olympic Games, fiddling while Rome burned, burning Christians to light up the night, building the vast Golden House, and so forth," Edward Champlin writes. " 'He had a longing,' we are told, 'for immortality and undying fame.' He succeeded, though not quite in the manner he intended, as he was transformed from the hero of his own story into the monster of history."[7]

Today, the very name Nero is a watchword for cruelty. He is associated with the persecution of defenseless people.

Yet there is also sadness in his life's story. His parents were horrible people. He was abandoned when he was only a few years old. When he became emperor, he was surrounded by people who told him what a great man he was. Yet at the end of his life, none of those people were left to stand by him. They'd been either alienated or eliminated. He died almost alone, cowering in terror.

The Jewish Revolt

At about the time Jesus was crucified, a group called the Zealots emerged among the Jews living in Judea, where Jesus had been born. At one time Judea had been independent, but for several decades it had been a Roman province. The Zealots wanted to restore Judea's independence.

Discontent was simmering in the province. Then in 66, an unpopular Roman official named Gessius Florus robbed the temple in Jerusalem of silver. The Jews rose up in open revolt. They wiped out the small Roman garrison, and then defeated a larger force that came in from the neighboring province of Syria. The second victory seemed to provide evidence that God was on their side—as He had appeared to be so many times in previous Jewish history. That led them to believe that they could achieve independence.

Vespasian

Despite his lack of interest in government, Nero knew that he couldn't allow that to happen. He ordered Vespasian, one of his best generals, to lead a massive Roman army into Judea and put down the rebellion. In the meantime, disagreements among Jewish leaders resulted in their followers' killing each other, which seriously undermined their ability to resist Vespasian as he advanced toward Jerusalem. Nero's death and Vespasian's eventual accession as emperor put a temporary halt to the campaign. It resumed in 70 with Vespasian's son Titus leading the Roman army into Jerusalem and destroying the temple following a long siege. Tens of thousands of Jews starved to death or were slaughtered. The survivors were sent away from their homeland as slaves. It was the end of a Jewish state until Israel was established in 1948.

The last Jewish holdouts escaped to the mountaintop fortress of Masada. In 73, a strong force of Romans besieged them and began building a ramp that inched its way to the top. On the night before the Romans were ready to break down the final barriers, the surrounded Jews committed mass suicide. Only a handful of women and children survived.

Chronology

A.D. 37   Born on December 15 in Antium, Italy (present-day Anzio), as Lucius Domitius Ahenobarbus

40   Father dies

47   Makes first public appearance

49   Mother, Agrippina, marries Claudius I; Lucius begins taking lessons from Seneca

50   Takes the name Nero

51   Wears the *toga virilis* for the first time

53   Marries Octavia

54   Becomes emperor on the death of his stepfather, Claudius I

55   Murders Claudius's son Britannicus

59   Orders Agrippina to be murdered

62   Orders the death of his wife, Octavia; marries Poppaea Sabina

63   Birth of daughter Claudia; she dies two months later

64   Begins the first persecution of Christians after blaming them for starting the fire that consumed much of Rome

65   Begins performing in public; orders Seneca to commit suicide; Poppaea dies from injuries sustained from his kicking her

66   Begins tour of Greece

67   Competes in Olympic Games

68   Is declared a public enemy and commits suicide

BIOGRAPHY FROM

ANCIENT CIVILIZATIONS

LEGENDS, FOLKLORE, AND STORIES OF ANCIENT WORLDS

Timeline in History

44 B.C.	Julius Caesar is assassinated in the Roman Senate.
27 B.C.	Octavian, Julius Caesar's designated heir, takes the name of Augustus Caesar and becomes the first Roman emperor.
4 B.C.	Roman statesman and playwright Seneca the Younger is born.
A.D. 9	Three Roman legions are annihilated at the Battle of Teutoburg Forest.
14	Augustus Caesar dies and is succeeded by Tiberius.
17	Ovid, the author of the long poem *Metamorphoses*, dies.
27	Jesus is baptized and begins his ministry.
30	Jesus is crucified.
37	Tiberius dies; his successor is his nephew Caligula.
40	One of the earliest Christian churches is built in Corinth, Greece.
41	Caligula is assassinated and Claudius I becomes emperor.
43	London, England, is founded by invading Roman troops; its original name is Londinium.
45	St. Paul begins his travels as a missionary; Nero will martyr him about 20 years later.
46	Greek biographer Plutarch is born.
58	Roman satirical poet Juvenal is born.
64	St. Peter is martyred by Nero.
69	Roman historian Suetonius is born; Vespasian becomes Roman emperor.
70	The Jewish revolt against Rome is suppressed; Jerusalem is destroyed and the Jews are sent into exile.
79	Vespasian dies; his son Titus succeeds him.
81	Titus dies; his brother Domitian becomes emperor.
96	Domitian is assassinated and Nerva becomes emperor.
98	After Nerva suffers a fatal stroke, his heir Trajan becomes emperor; the Roman Empire reaches its greatest extent during his reign.
117	Trajan dies.

BIOGRAPHY FROM
ANCIENT CIVILIZATIONS
LEGENDS, FOLKLORE, AND STORIES OF ANCIENT WORLDS

Chapter Notes

CHAPTER ONE   I AM THE CHAMPION

  1. Edward Champlin, *Nero* (Cambridge, MA: Harvard University Press, 2003), p. 53.

CHAPTER TWO   THE TEENAGED EMPEROR

  1. Suetonius, *The Twelve Caesars*, translated by Robert Graves (New York: Penguin Books, 1957), pp. 224–25.

  2. Richard Holland, *Nero: The Man Behind the Myth* (Phoenix Mill, Thrupp, Stroud, United Kingdom: Sutton Publishing, 2000), p. 57–58.

  3. Suetonius, p. 211.

  4. Phil Grabsky, *I, Caesar: Ruling the Roman Empire* (London: BBC Books, 1997), p. 104.

CHAPTER THREE   BECOMING INDEPENDENT

  1. Michael Grant, *Nero: Emperor in Revolt* (New York: American Heritage Press, 1970), p. 41.

CHAPTER FOUR   FROM MURDERER TO MUSICIAN

  1. Richard Holland, *Nero: The Man Behind the Myth* (Phoenix Mill, Thrupp, Stroud, United Kingdom: Sutton Publishing, 2000), p. 100.

  2. Suetonius, *The Twelve Caesars*, translated by Robert Graves (New York: Penguin Books, 1957), p. 222.

CHAPTER FIVE   A LONELY DEATH

  1. Suetonius, *The Twelve Caesars*, translated by Robert Graves (New York: Penguin Books, 1957), p. 229.

  2. Ibid., p. 225.

  3. Phil Grabsky, *I, Caesar: Ruling the Roman Empire* (London: BBC Books, 1997), p. 126.

  4. Ibid., pp. 129–30.

  5. Suetonius, p. 224.

  6. Edward Champlin, *Nero* (Cambridge, MA: Harvard University Press, 2003), p. 5.

  7. Ibid., pp. 236–37.

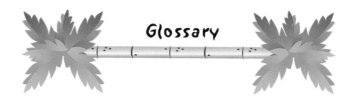

BIOGRAPHY FROM
ANCIENT CIVILIZATIONS
LEGENDS, FOLKLORE, AND STORIES OF ANCIENT WORLDS

Glossary

bureaucracy	(byoo-ROCK-ruh-see)—administration of a government through several departments, or bureaus.
essayist	(EH-say-ist)—a person who writes essays, literary compositions that often reflect a personal point of view.
exile	(EK-zile)—to force a person to leave his or her home country and live somewhere else.
freedman	(FREED-man)—a person who has been freed from slavery.
forum	(FORE-um)—the administrative and commercial center of an ancient Roman city.
legions	(LEE-juns)—the primary divisions of the Roman army, each containing about 5,000 men.
lyre	(LIAR)—a small stringed instrument, similar to a harp, used to accompany recitations of poetry or other literature.
purge	(PERJ)—to get rid of people considered to be dangerous.
strigil	(STRY-jel)—curved device made of bronze, used to scrape dirt and moisture off the skin.
sycophants	(SIH-kuh-fants)—people showing an especially high degree of flattery.
toga	(TOE-guh)—one-piece draped garment worn by Roman citizens.

BIOGRAPHY FROM
ANCIENT CIVILIZATIONS
LEGENDS, FOLKLORE, AND STORIES OF ANCIENT WORLDS

For Further Reading

For Young Adults

Hicks, Peter. *Gods and Goddesses in the Daily Life of the Ancient Romans.* Columbus, OH: Peter Bedrick Books, 2003.

James, Simon. *Ancient Rome.* New York: Viking, 1992.

Mantin, Peter, and Richard Pulley. *The Roman World: From Republic to Empire.* Cambridge, England: Cambridge University Press, 1992.

Morgan, Julian. *Nero: Destroyer of Rome.* New York: Rosen Publishing Group, 2003.

Powers, Elizabeth. *Nero.* Broomall, PA: Chelsea House Publishing, 1988.

Sheehan, Sean. *Ancient Rome.* Austin, TX: Raintree Steck-Vaughn, 2000.

Works Consulted

Champlin, Edward. *Nero.* Cambridge, MA: Harvard University Press, 2003.

Grabsky, Phil. *I, Caesar: Ruling the Roman Empire.* London: BBC Books, 1997.

Grant, Michael. *History of Rome.* New York: Charles Scribner's Sons, 1978.

———. *Nero: Emperor in Revolt.* New York: American Heritage Press, 1970.

Holland, Richard. *Nero: The Man Behind the Myth.* Phoenix Mill, Thrupp, Stroud, United Kingdom: Sutton Publishing, 2000.

Klingaman, William K. *The First Century.* New York: HarperCollins, 1990.

Perrottet, Tony. *The Naked Olympics.* New York: Random House Trade Paperbacks, 2004.

Suetonius. *The Twelve Caesars.* Translated by Robert Graves. New York: Penguin Books, 1957.

On the Internet

Ancient/Classical History, "Nero— Eyewitness Accounts"
http://ancienthistory.miningco.com/cs/neroeyewitness/index.htm

BBC: Historic Figures, "Nero (A.D. 37– 68, Roman emperor A.D. 54–68)"
http://www.bbc.co.uk/history/historic_figures/nero.shtml

De Imperatoribus Romanis: An Online Encyclopedia of Roman Emperors
http://www.roman-emperors.org

PBS: *The Roman Empire in the First Century*
http://www.pbs.org/empires/romans/index.html

Index